Contents

Well done, Ben and Lucy!

1 **Look at the pictures and letters. Write the words.**

1 greathophopr

photographer

2 routjailns

3 pcomeiorhn

4 dabn

5 mogded scar

6 recrostlloare

7 bgi lhewe

8 robotduuan

9 ymrao

2 **Read and write the words.**

1 She writes stories for newspapers.   *journalist*

2 He's the most important man in town.

3 She takes photos.

4 They play music.

5 You speak into this.

6 Four fairground rides:

1 Match the questions with the answers.

1. Are you eleven?
2. What's your favourite colour?
3. When do you get up in the mornings?
4. Where do you go on your holidays?
5. Who is your best friend?
6. Do you like going on adventures with Ben?
7. Does Ben ever make you angry?
8. Is it fun being an Explorer?

a ☐ Yes, it is.

b ☐ Ben, of course.

c ☐ Yes, I do.

d ☐ Blue, definitely.

e ☐ Sometimes, when he's scared of silly things.

f ☐ Half past seven.

g [1] No, I'm ten.

h ☐ I go to the beach.

2 Read and complete the questions.

1. _How_ old are you?
2. _____ do you live?
3. _____ you got any brothers or sisters?
4. _____ your favourite colour red?
5. _____ your school got a uniform?
6. _____ is your favourite subject?
7. _____ do you get home from school?
8. _____ you tell your best friend everything?

3 Answer the questions from Activity 2 about yourself.

1. _____
2. _____
3. _____
4. _____
5. _____
6. _____
7. _____
8. _____

1 **Remember the song. Write the words in order.**

fun. / Here / they / ~~The~~ / come. / and /
Adventure / and / Lucy / ~~Explorers.~~ / Ben.

The Explorers.

_____

_____

_____

stars. / Ben / are. / Here / The / and /
Action / they / Lucy. / Explorers.

_____

_____

_____

_____

2 **Is it Ben or Lucy in the song? Write the sentences on the T-shirts.**

I find a lot of treasure.   I like adventure.
I love exploring things.   I'm not scared of anything.

3 **Answer the questions.**

Are you an Explorer?

1 Do you like adventure? _____

2 Do you like exploring things? _____

3 Do you like exciting things? _____

4 Are you scared of anything? _____

Key
Q 1–3: yes = 1 point, no = 0 points
Q 4: no = 1 point, yes = 0 points

4 points: You're a true Explorer, just like Ben and Lucy.

3 points: You're nearly an Explorer.

1–2 points: You aren't an Explorer at the moment.

0 points: You aren't really an Explorer.

1 **CD 1 10** **What did Emma do at the party? Listen and tick (✓).**

2 **Read and complete the questions.**

1 What _was_ the party like?

2 _____ there a band?

3 _____ you dance?

4 _____ there a barbecue?

5 _____ you have a lot of fun?

6 _____ there dodgems too?

3 **Write questions for the answers.**

1 _What did you do last night_ ?

Last night? I watched TV.

2 _____ ?

I watched a film.

3 _____ ?

Yes, it was a really good film.

4 _____ ?

No, I didn't watch the match. I don't like football.

5 _____ ?

No, I didn't do my homework. I'm going to do it at the weekend.

6 _____ ?

I went to bed at about 10 o'clock.

1 Think! Remember the story. Put the sentences in order.

☐ Mr Davidson tells them about a king.

1 The children tell Mr Davidson about their adventure.

☐ Mr Davidson shows the children a map.

☐ Mr Davidson finds a symbol on the statue.

☐ Horax phones Zelda.

☐ The children see the symbol and read a rhyme on the map.

2 Read and write the words.

| go   rhyme   quiz   is   ~~know~~   find |

Study the map, so then you (1) _know_ the places where you have to (2)_____ .

When you get there, look and (3)_____ a line like this to make a (4)_____ .

The lines together make a (5)_____ to tell you where the treasure (6)_____ .

3 Think! The pictures on the map tell Ben and Lucy where to look. Look, guess and write sentences. Use words from the box.

| school   library   zoo   lake   station   ~~museum~~   concert hall
castle   statue   art gallery   restaurant   planetarium |

①

I think they have to
find a museum.

②

③

④

⑤

⑥

1 Match the rhyming words.

① noise ② rhyme ③ shoe ④ toe ⑤ cheese

ⓐ trees ⓑ snow ⓒ boys ⓓ time ⓔ glue

2 (CD 1 13) Listen, say and check your answers.

3 (Think!) Which one is different in each group? Read, think and circle.

1	dodgem car	(microphone)	roundabout	big wheel
2	code	book	newspaper	treasure
3	journalist	mayor	photographer	rollercoaster
4	had	opened	wanted	used
5	famous	exciting	reading	dangerous

4 Colour the bricks to make sentences. Write in the missing words.

1	_Does_ your	you go on	in a band?
2	_____ your parents	TV	yesterday?
3	Where _____	brother play	the weekend?
4	_____ you watch	you do at	Spanish?
5	_____ did	speak	holiday last summer?

⑴ In the museum

1 **Complete the words. Then draw lines.**

a

b

c

d

e

1 s w o r d
2 h __ l m __ t
3 s __ i e __ d
4 bo __ and a r r __ w
5 __ n i __ h t

6 n __ c k l a __ e
7 c r o __ n
8 b e __ t
9 q __ e e __
10 b __ a __ e l e t

f

g

h

i

j

2 **Look, read and number the sentences.**

1   2   3   4   5   6

a ⟨2⟩ She's wearing a dress, a crown and two bracelets.

b ⟨ ⟩ He's wearing a helmet. He's carrying a shield and a bow and arrow.

c ⟨ ⟩ He's wearing a helmet. He's carrying a shield and a sword.

d ⟨ ⟩ She's wearing a dress with a belt, a crown and a bracelet.

e ⟨ ⟩ She's wearing a dress, a crown, a necklace and a bracelet.

f ⟨ ⟩ He's carrying his helmet. He's wearing his sword on his belt.

1 **Write the sentences under the pictures.**

> I must drink more water.   I mustn't touch my sister's CDs.
> I must take off my shoes in the house.   I mustn't eat too much ice cream.
> I must do my homework.   ~~I mustn't run in the living room.~~

1

I mustn't run in the
living room.

2

3

4

5

6

2 **Read and write _must_ or _mustn't_ and a word from the box.**

> shout   keep   use   ~~wear~~   drink   buy

1 I _must_ _wear_ a helmet when I ride my bike. It keeps my head safe.

2 I _____ _____ in the house when my baby brother is sleeping.

3 I _____ _____ water from the lake. It's dirty.

4 I _____ _____ the dog on his lead. I don't want him to chase cats.

5 I _____ _____ a new T-shirt. I've got too many already!

6 I _____ _____ my camera here. The sign says 'No photos'.

3 **What must or mustn't you do at home or at school?**
Write four sentences: two with _must_ and two with _mustn't_.

I must wear school uniform.

1 What does the knight say? What mustn't he do in the museum? Look and write sentences.

1
I mustn't

2

3

2 Remember the song. Correct the sentences.

1 The bracelets are in the vase. The bracelets are flying round.
2 The necklaces are flying round.
3 The crowns are on the ground.
4 The swords are roaring.
5 The vase is fighting.
6 The lions are shouting.

3 Describe the scene at the museum.

It's midnight at the museum. The knight is dancing.

1 **Read and circle.**

1 Please help <u>Bob</u>.   （him）/ he

2 Please show the photo to <u>Jenna</u>.   she / her

3 Please write <u>Ruby and me</u> an email.   us / we

4 Tell the story to <u>Frank and Amy</u>.   they / them

5 Buy a new dress for <u>Mia</u>.   her / she

6 Please give the pen to <u>Jack</u>.   he / him

2 **Change the sentences.**

1 Don't tell Hannah.
   Don't tell her.

2 Don't show the letter to Joel and Frank.

3 Don't give any money to Ryan.

4 Don't take the apples!

5 Please don't shout at Bella and me.

6 Don't give any bananas to Ella.

1 Remember the story. Read and write *t* (true) or *f* (false).

1 Someone is trying to hurt Lucy and Ben with a shield. f

2 The knight comes after them.

3 The knight finds Lucy and Ben.

4 The knight falls down the stairs.

5 Lucy and Ben find a rhyme on the knight's sword.

6 The knight was Zelda.

2 Read and write the words.

chase   queen   children   knight   dressing   going

Zelda,
I'm (1) _dressing_ up as the (2)_____ ! When the (3)_____
come into the museum, I'm (4)_____ to scare them. Then I'm
going to (5)_____ them. You can be the (6)_____ .
Horax

3 Think!   Draw lines and complete the sentences.

1 The dinosaur _is from the Nature Museum_ .

2 The owl _____ .

3 The motorbike _____ .

4 The shield _____ .

5 The plane _____ .

6 The knight _____ .

1 **CD1 23** **Listen and write the missing words. Then say with a friend.**

1

Tim: Look out!

Sue: What was that?

Tim: The tree. It just fell.

Sue: Wow! _____

_____ _____ !

2

Liam: What am I going to buy you for your birthday?

Kim: _____ _____

_____ _____ !

Liam: What?

Kim: Nothing! That's what you bought me last year!

2 **Colour the squares yell*ow* or br*ow*n.**

yellow	brown	bow and arrow	crown
know	window	how	town
show	now	flower	snow

3 **CD1 24** **Listen, say and check your answers.**

1 **Values** **What can we learn from the story? Colour the words.**

Knowing   Talking   a lot   can't   can

find   help   you   I   in   out

your   their   life   name   .

2 **Read and write the words.**

> case   daughter   torch   checked   ~~interesting~~   locked   piece   key

1 Mr Benson told children _interesting_ stories.

2 The best _____ in the museum was a statue of a gold cat.

3 The statue was in a glass _____ .

4 When Mr Benson went home, he always _____ the windows and the doors.

5 He had an eighteen-year-old _____ called Cleo.

6 After the party, Mr Benson took the _____ to the museum and closed the window.

7 He _____ the alarm.

8 When Cleo heard a noise, she waited and then she switched on her _____ .

3 **Think!** **Draw the missing symbol in Box 3.**

Listen and draw a line from the day to the correct picture.

Monday

Tuesday

Wednesday

History

Thursday

Friday

Saturday

Sunday

1 **Read and write the words.**

collection   exhibits   galleries   ~~ancient~~

1 very old _ancient_
2 objects in a museum _____
3 a group of objects that are the same _____
4 rooms in a museum _____

2 (Values) **Read the story. What can we learn from it? Tick (✓).**

My grandpa likes to tell me stories about when he was young.
We live in the city, but when my grandpa was a boy, he lived
on a farm high up in the mountains.

   When we go shopping, we get into the car and drive
to the supermarket. We do the shopping, put it in the car
and drive home.

   When my grandpa went shopping, he walked down the
mountain, then he bought things in a small shop in a village,
he put them in his rucksack and then he walked back to the
farm again. He didn't buy very much, just the things which
they didn't have at the farm, such as flour, oil and salt.

On the farm they baked their own bread. One day
my grandpa took me to a museum. There they showed us
how to bake bread. My grandpa said, 'That's how we baked
our bread on the farm.' We tasted the bread in the museum
and it was really nice.

Last winter I went skiing with my family and we stayed
in a hut in the mountains. For the first few days, there was
a lot of sun and we skied, but then it snowed for three days.
It was too dangerous to leave the hut and soon we had
no more bread. Then I remembered my grandpa. 'I can bake
bread,' I said to my parents, but they didn't believe me.

   We had water, oil and salt, and luckily we found some flour in a cupboard.
I remembered what my grandpa told me and baked some bread. It wasn't
really very nice, but everybody liked it because they were hungry.

☐ We cannot learn anything from history.
☐ We can never do the same things which people did a long time ago.
☐ We can learn a lot from history.

1 **Think!** Archaeologists found these objects. What did people use them for? Listen and number the pictures.

a b c d e f

a ☐ b ☐ c ☐ d 1 e ☐ f ☐

2 Look, read and write the words.

> big   didn't   fruit   gardening   Germany   loved   know   ~~tried~~

Giant Shoe Museum, Washington, USA

British Lawnmower Museum, Merseyside, UK

Banana Museum, Washington, USA

German Sausage Museum, Thuringia, Germany

1 I _tried_____ a pair, but they were too _____ for me.

2 Dad loves _____ so we went to this museum, but I _____ like it.

3 There was everything that you want to _____ about this _____ !

4 My brother _____ this museum in _____ . He loves meat.

1 **Match the questions with the answers.**

1 When did you leave the museum?

2 What did you do outside?

3 Did you go back in the morning?

4 So what did you do?

5 Did you like it outside?

6 Are you going to go out again?

a ☐ No, I didn't. The window was closed.

b ☐ I don't think so. Mr Benson said, 'I mustn't forget to close the windows.'

c ☐1 Three nights ago when Mr Benson forgot to close a window.

d ☐ I met another cat and we hunted rats.

e ☐ Yes, it was great.

f ☐ I waited and the next night someone opened the window.

2 **Look at Activity 1. <u>Underline</u> the mistakes. Then write the correct sentences.**

One night Mr Benson <u>left a door open</u>. The Egyptian cat got out of its glass case.

Outside, it met a dog. When the Egyptian cat wanted to get back in, the door was locked. She waited and two nights later someone opened a window. She went back into her glass case.

One night Mr Benson left a window open.

_____

_____

_____

3 **Imagine that a different exhibit escaped. Write what happened.**

● Which exhibit escaped?

● What did it do outside?

● When did it go back to the museum?

One day Mr Benson left the window open again. The

1 Write the words in three groups.

ancient belt bow and arrow bracelet collection crown
exhibits galleries helmet necklace shield sword

1 ancient

2 belt

3 bow and arrow

2 Look at Activity 1. Number the topics to match the groups.

☐ For fighting ☐ Museum words ☐ For wearing

3 Look and draw lines to make sentences.

1 Give

us	the	balls	yesterday, please.
them	a	shoes	tomorrow, please.
me	an	ball	now, please.

2 You

aren't	make	silence	in the museum.
mustn't	be	photos	in the shop.
must	take	a noise	in the zoo.

3 You

must	brush	your hair	before bed.
have	wash	your face	after bed.
mustn't	dry	your teeth	in bed.

4 The dog

is	hungry.	Give me	some water, please.
am	thirsty.	Give them	any more, please.
are	tired.	Give him	no more, please.

② The world around us

1 Find and write eight words. Look →, ↓ and ↘.

1 _field_

2 _____

m	f	r	i	p	l	a	k	r	u
o	p	s	f	s	a	p	g	i	z
u	e	f	i	t	n	t	j	v	f
n	b	o	e	l	d	e	h	e	o
t	v	i	l	l	a	g	e	r	r
a	r	i	d	f	o	k	p	a	e
i	s	l	a	n	d	s	e	f	s
n	a	v	i	l	i	v	e	r	t

3 _____

4 _____

5 _____

6 _____

7 _____

8 _____

2 Read and write words from Activity 1.

1 **A:** Can we swim to that _island_ in the middle of the lake?

    B: No, you can't, but look, we can all go on that boat.

2 **A:** I can see some lights there. Is that a town?

    B: No, there are only a few houses. It's a _____ .

3 **A:** Let's go through the trees.

    B: No, I think we should stay on the _____ . It's safer.

4 **A:** How can we get across the _____ ?

    B: Look, there's a bridge.

5 **A:** Why can't we go into that _____ ?

    B: Because they're cutting down some trees. It's too dangerous.

1 Find and write four sentences.

1 It was a lovely day, so Jane and Daisy wanted to have a picnic.

2 _____

3 _____

4 _____

2 Join the sentences with *and*, *but*, *so* and *because*.

1 There are fields near our village. People love having picnics there.

   There are fields near our village and people love having picnics there.

2 It started to rain. We went home.

3 John went to the USA. He stayed in Chicago.

4 Kate liked visiting her uncle. It took two hours by car.

5 The film was boring. We left the cinema.

6 Don't go across that old bridge. It's dangerous.

3 Write four sentences about you. Use *and*, *but*, *so* and *because*.

I like watching football and ...   I like watching football, but ...

1 **Remember the song. Complete the lines.**

Walking with Mum
Is so much (1) _fun_ .
Walking with Mum
In the morning (2) _____ .

We got up very early.
What a lovely (3) _____ !
We walked through some villages,
Singing all the (4) _____ .

'Let's sit here,' said Mum
And pointed to some (5) _____ .
'We can have a picnic –
I've got some bread and (6) _____ .'
Walking with Mum ...

We walked through the fields,
But that was a (7) _____ .
Mum didn't see the path
And fell into the (8) _____ !

The water was so cold,
Mum's face was (9) _____
And so she caught a cold.
Atchoo! (10) _____ !
Walking with Mum ...

2 **Complete Mum's email to her friend Sally.**

| Send | Chat | Attach | Address | Format | Save | – ⬜ ✕ |

To: _____
Subject: _____

Dear Sally,

Yesterday the children wanted to go walking with me. We got up
early. It was a lovely day and _____
_____
_____
_____

See you soon, _____

Caroline _____

1 **Look at Superman and Superwoman's photo album. What could they do 40 years ago? Write sentences. Use the words from the box.**

> lift up (x 2)   ~~fight with~~   run faster than (x 2)   ride on   jump from   climb

1   40 years ago, Superman could fight with a crocodile.
2   _____
3   _____
4   _____
5   _____
6   _____
7   _____
8   _____

2 **What can you do now that you couldn't do when you were younger? Write sentences.**

When I was three, I couldn't read and write.
_____
_____
_____

1 **Remember the story. Read and write the words.**

saw   was   helped   pocket   hungry
village   missing   ~~walk~~   waiter   menu

Ben and Lucy went for a great (1) _walk_ with Ben's grandpa. When they felt (2) _____ , Grandpa took them to a lovely restaurant in a little (3) _____ . Buster (4) _____ hungry too. At the restaurant Grandpa (5) _____ that Ben and Lucy had a map. Ben and Lucy wanted to tell Ben's grandpa about it, but the (6) _____ came and brought the soup, so Ben put the map in his (7) _____ . Later, Ben found out that the map was (8) _____ . Grandpa said, 'I didn't like the waiter very much, so I put a (9) _____ in your pocket and kept the map.' Then Grandpa (10) _____ the children to find the symbol and the line of the rhyme.

2 **Think!** **Make words with the letters of *restaurant*.**

aunt, run, _____

_____

3 **Think!** **Complete the waiter's diary entry.**

Today there was an (1) _old man_ in the restaurant. He was with two (2) _____ . They (3) _____ for lunch. When I took the soup, I saw (4) _____ on the table. I wanted to know about it, so I took (5) _____ to their table. One child said the next picture on the map was (6) _____ , but the other one said that you don't find (7) _____ . I took the map with me, but when I looked at it in the kitchen, I saw that it (8) _____ . I think the old man took the map and put the menu (9) _____ . I was very (10) _____ !

1 CD 1 38 **Listen and write the missing words. Then say with a friend.**

1

Jen: Mr Price, this is for your new house.

Mr Price: _____ _____

_____ plant! Thank you! That's very kind.

2

Dawn: Did you see those two men in the car?

Dan: Yes. What about them?

Dawn: _____ _____

_____ _____

_____ them.

Dan: What do you mean?

Dawn: One had a T-shirt and shorts and the other had a big winter coat and boots!

2 **Make sentences. Then circle the silent consonants.**

1	The knight's	a	☐	knows about volcanoes.
2	Please write	b	☐	answer.
3	The scientist	c	1	got a sword.
4	The rhinos live	d	☐	listen to the teacher.
5	That's the wrong	e	☐	a rhyme in your notebooks.
6	At school you must	f	☐	on an island.

3 CD 1 39 **Listen, say and check your answers.**

1 ^{CD1} **Listen and write _t_ (true) or _f_ (false).**

1 For her birthday party, Kate invited three friends. | f |

2 One of her presents was a book about butterflies. | |

3 Kate's favourite present was her new pencil case. | |

4 At half past nine, Dad took the children for a night walk. | |

5 The wind in the trees sounded like animals. | |

6 Kate's uncle and dad played a trick on her. | |

2 **Write the story. Use the pictures and the sentences from Activity 1 to help you.**

It was Kate's birthday. She invited her friend Lisa to the party.

3 (Values) **What can we learn from the story? Tick (✓).**

☐ Spending money on presents is important.

☐ Spending time with your friends and family is important.

☐ Having a party is important.

1 Look and read. Write 1, 2 or 3 words to complete the sentences about the story.

Hide and sleep

Last week Mum and Dad took us to the furniture shop. They wanted to buy a new sofa because our old one wasn't very comfortable. My brother and I weren't very happy because we don't really like shopping, but then Mum said that Grandpa wanted to come too. We liked that idea because Grandpa is cool!

The shop was really big. Mum and Dad left us with Grandpa and went to look at furniture. Grandpa had a brilliant idea. 'This shop is very big,' he said, 'so let's have a game of hide and seek.' We were really excited because there were so many places to hide. My brother hid first and after ten minutes

I found him behind a cupboard. Then it was my turn, but Grandpa found me very quickly. Finally, it was Grandpa's turn. We closed our eyes and counted to 100. 'Coming!' we shouted. We looked and we looked, but we couldn't find Grandpa anywhere. After half an hour, Mum and Dad came back. 'Where's Grandpa?' they asked. Now all the family started to look for him. When we were in the part of the shop where they had beds, we heard a funny noise. 'Shhh!' said Dad. 'Someone is snoring.' We looked across the shop and there on the most comfortable bed was Grandpa – asleep!

1 The family went shopping for _a new sofa_____ .

2 The children really like their _____ .

3 Grandpa wanted to play _____ .

4 It took them _____ to find the first person.

5 _____ the last person to hide.

6 After _____ minutes, their parents came back.

7 The family heard _____ .

8 They found Grandpa in the shop, sleeping on the _____ .

1 **Look at the paintings. Write five sentences. Use the words from the box or your own ideas.**

> most beautiful   most modern   oldest
> most difficult to understand   most interesting

I think painting number 2 is the …

I like number 4 best because …

I don't like number 1, but … because …

Think! **Read Danny's text and think. Which picture is he describing?**

I think this is a beautiful picture and it's very interesting. It isn't easy to understand at first. When I look at it for a long time, this is what I imagine: there's a river with a high waterfall and there's a fish in the lake at the bottom. The water is very fast.

Picture ☐

  Look and imagine. What do you see? Write about the other picture from Activity 1.

1 **Match the questions with the answers.**

1 What do you prefer doing in your free time, Isabel?

2 What activities do you like doing outdoors?

3 And what do you like doing at home?

4 Do you spend a lot of time on the Internet?

5 What about being in town? Do you like that?

6 Do you like going to shops?

a ☐ I love walking, watching birds and helping in the garden.

b ☐ Not very much because there are too many cars and it's noisy.

c ☐ Yes, I use it every day to look for information and I write emails.

d ☐ I love reading a lot. When I have a good book, I can't stop. I never watch TV.

e ☐ Yes, I do. Sometimes I go with Mum and we have lots of fun.

f ☐ 1 When the weather is nice, I prefer being outdoors. When it rains, I love staying at home.

2 **Look at Activity 1. <u>Underline</u> the mistakes. Then write the correct sentences.**

> Isabel is very much an outdoor person. She <u>likes riding her bike</u>. She also likes listening to birds and sleeping in the garden. When the weather is nice, she loves being at home. She watches a lot of TV. She never uses a computer so she doesn't send emails. Isabel doesn't like being in town very much. She thinks that there are too many people.

She loves walking.

_____

_____

_____

3 **Write about your free time.**

I'm an outdoor person.

1 (Think!) **Which one is different in each group? Look, think and circle.**

1

2

3

2 **Colour the bricks to make sentences. Write in the missing words.**

1	He liked the book	was young,	they saw a snake.
2	They were scared	and	write.
3	When Grandma	two, I _____	she _____ run really fast.
4	When I was	_____	went to bed.
5	She was tired,	_____ she	he _couldn't_ stop reading it!

3 Danger!

1 Complete the words.

1 f i r e
2 _ m b _ l _ n c _
3 fl _ _ d
4 p _ l _ c _   c _ r
5 p _ r _ m _ d _ c

6 f _ r _ f _ ght _ r
7 p _ l _ c _   _ ff _ c _ r
8 f _ r _   _ ng _ n _
9 _ m _ rg _ ncy s _ rv _ c _ s

2 Complete the diagram with the words from Activity 1.

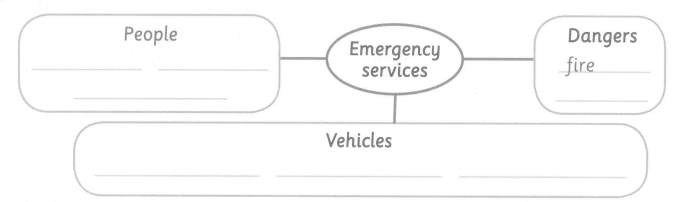

People

Emergency services

Dangers
fire

Vehicles

3 Read and complete the text. Use the words from Activity 2.

One day I was on my way to school and I saw smoke. It was coming out of a house. I had my mobile phone, so I called the (1) _emergency services_ . Five minutes later, a big red (2) _____ came down the road. It stopped and four (3) _____ got out. It was really exciting. They started to fight the (4) _____ and there was water everywhere! It was like a (5) _____ . Then an (6) _____ arrived with two (7) _____ but there wasn't anyone in the house, so they went back to the hospital. Finally two (8) _____ arrived. 'Do you live here?' one of them asked me. 'No, I don't,' I said, 'but I called 999.' 'That's good,' the other one said, 'but you should be at school now. What school do you go to?' 'Castle Park,' I answered. 'OK, we can take you,' one of them said … and I got a ride in a (9) _____ !

1 **Write *was* or *were*.**

Yesterday at 11 o'clock in the park,

1 … Tim _was_ riding his bike,

2 … Mr Brown _____ reading a newspaper,

3 … Ian and Ruth _____ playing football,

4 … my dog _____ chasing a ball,

5 … Sara _____ running

6 … and Mr and Mrs Smith _____ walking their dog.

2 **Describe the picture. Use the words from the box.**

| talk   fight   try   sing   ~~watch~~ |

Yesterday at eight o'clock,

1 … Mum and Dad _were watching TV_ _____ ,

2 … my brother _____ ,

3 … my sister _____ ,

4 … the dog and the cat _____

5 … and I _____ to do my homework!

1 Remember the song. Look and number the objects.

 1

 2

 3

 4

 5

b ☐

a ☐

c ☐

d ☐

e 1

2 Complete the sentences.

1 Dad _was fixing the lights_____ .

2 Emily was _____ .

3 Jonathan was _____ .

4 I was _____ .

5 Mum was _____ .

3 Think! What were these people doing? Imagine and write sentences.

1 Grandma _____ .

2 Aunt Vicky _____ .

3 Cousin Bob _____ .

4 The baby _____ .

3

1 Match the questions with the answers.

1 What was Jack doing at 7 o'clock?
2 What were you and Sue doing?
3 What was the cat doing?
4 What was Jill doing at 8 o'clock?
5 What were you doing?
6 What were Bill and Liz doing?

a ☐ I was doing my homework.
b ☐1 He was playing computer games.
c ☐ They were playing cards.
d ☐ It was sleeping.
e ☐ We were watching TV.
f ☐ She was listening to music.

2 Look and write questions for the answers.

Grandma   Grandpa   Nathan and Jacob   Dad

1 What _was Grandma doing at 3 o'clock_ ?
She was gardening.

2 _____ , Grandpa?
I was reading a book.

3 _____ ?
They were riding their bikes.

4 _____ ?
He was cooking.

3 Read the questions and answers. Answer the questions about yourself.

What was Bea's family doing ...	Her little brother and sister ...	You
... at 6 o'clock?	... were sleeping.	I was sleeping.
... at 7 o'clock?	... were playing.	
... at 8 o'clock?	... were having breakfast.	
... at 9 o'clock?	... were having a swimming lesson with Mum.	
... at 10 o'clock?	... were arriving at the shops.	

1 **Think!** **Remember the story. Read and circle.**

1 Why does Ben's grandpa say, 'Stay in the car, please?
   A   Because he wants Lucy to talk to the operator.
   B   Because it's too dangerous for them.
2 Why does the operator ask Lucy about the house number?
   A   Because she wants to know where Lucy lives.
   B   Because she's going to send an ambulance and a fire engine there.
3 Why does Ben's grandpa say to the man, 'Quick! We must get you out'?
   A   Because the man's leg hurts.
   B   Because it's dangerous to stay in the car after the accident.
4 Why does Ben's grandpa say, 'Don't go so fast'?
   A   Because the man on the motorbike is a dangerous driver.
   B   Because the man on the motorbike is making them wet.

2 **Think!** **How useful are these people? Write 2, 1 or 0.**

2 points = very useful   1 point = quite useful   0 points = not useful at all

a   0

Help! It's terrible! Please help! Come here!

b

Hello. This is John Brown. I'm in Station Road opposite the supermarket. There's an accident. There's a man. He can't walk.

c

Hi, this is Betty Miller. I'm in West Street. There's a car on fire and ... it looks dangerous.

d

Wow! An accident, look! Climb up here and you can see it better!

1 CD2 12 **Listen and write the missing words. Then say with a friend.**

①

Zak: Where are you going?

Alien: Back to my planet.

Zak: _____

_____

_____ ?

Alien: Of course you can.

Zak: Great, but I need to be back for tea at 6 o'clock.

②

May: There was an accident outside our house last night! We were watching TV and _____

_____ _____ _____

loud noise. I ran to the window and saw two cars.

Liam: Did you call the police?

May: No, I didn't because I could see that no-one was hurt … and one of them was a police car!

2 **Complete the words.**

1 kn*ight*_____

2 wh_____

3 l_____ning

4 midn_____

5 firef_____er

6 k_____

3 CD2 13 **Listen, say and check your answers.**

1 Values **What can we learn from the story? Colour the words.**

Quick   Slow   listening   thinking

can   help   escape   to

save   people   water   .

2 **Answer the questions. Use your imagination.**

Imagine it is 24 December 2004. Think about these questions:

- Where is Tilly?   • What is the weather like?   • What is she doing?

Now use your answers to complete Tilly's postcard.

Dear Rachel,
I'm having a fantastic time here in
_____
_____

_____
I can't wait for Christmas tomorrow!
Lots of love,
Tilly

3 **Write another postcard from Tilly on 28 December 2004.**

Tilly tells Rachel:

- where she is
- what happened
- what she did
- what she is going to do now

1 **Look and read. Choose the correct words and write them on the lines.**

a hut

a hotel

a snorkel

a sandcastle

1 This is a building. You stay here when you are on holiday.   *a hotel*

2 This is very cold. You eat it and it tastes sweet.

3 You can breathe under water with this.

4 This is a very big wave. It is very dangerous.

5 This is a small building. Some are houses. Some are shops.

6 Children like to build this on the beach.

7 This is a person who is on holiday.

a tourist

a beach ball

a tsunami

an ice cream

2 **Find six differences. Write sentences.**

A

B

In picture A the sandcastle is …

(Values) **Read the story. What can we learn from it? Tick (✓).**

1

Tara: What's that funny smell?
Matt: Oh, no … the house is on fire.
Follow me and do exactly what I say.

2

Tara: I must get my teddy bear!
Matt: Where is he?
Tara: Upstairs, of course. In my bedroom.
Matt: I'm sorry – it's too dangerous.

3

Tara: I can't breathe with all this smoke.
Matt: Don't worry. Get down on your knees
like this and crawl.

4

Matt: There isn't as much smoke here.
Tara: Can I stand up?
Matt: Yes, but let me close the door to stop
the fire. Let's get to the back door.

5

Tara: Are we safe now?
Matt: Yes, we are, but let's get away from
the house. I'm going to phone the emergency
services.

6

Firefighter: Well done! Your actions saved
your lives and most of your house.
Matt: Thanks. It was something that they
taught us at school.
Tara: Teddy! You're alive!

☐ When there's a fire, take photos of it.

☐ When you smell smoke, open the window.

☐ Knowing what to do in a fire can save lives.

1 **Read and draw the escape routes.**

From my bedroom: go downstairs and out of the front door.
If the fire is on the stairs, go to my parents' room and climb
onto the kitchen roof.

2 **Think!** **Draw escape plans for your house.**

3 **Write escape plans from:**

- your bedroom
- the kitchen
- the living room

[ ] **B:** When is it going to arrive?

[ ] **A:** Good, so you're safe. Is there anyone in number 37?

[ ] **B:** I'm calling from 39 Grange Road. The fire's at number 37.

[1] **A:** Hello. How can we help you?

[ ] **B:** Yes, I am.

[ ] **A:** OK. Don't go in to check. Stay and wait for the fire engine.

[ ] **B:** I'm calling to report a house fire next door to us.

[ ] **A:** In about five minutes. Don't worry and keep a safe distance.

[ ] **A:** Where are you calling from?

[ ] **B:** I'm not sure.

[ ] **A:** And are you outside the house?

2 **Look and write a dialogue. Use language from Activity 1.**

Hello, how can we help you? _____

_____

_____

_____

_____

_____

_____

_____

1 Write the words in four groups.

~~accident~~ ~~ambulance~~ ~~banana cake~~ fire fire engine flood
~~hut~~ ice cream police car sandcastle snorkel vanilla shake

1
accident
_____

2
ambulance
_____

3
banana cake
_____

4
hut
_____

2 Look at Activity 1. Number the topics to match the groups.

☐ Dangers   ☐ Emergency services

☐ On the beach   ☐ Food words

3 Look and draw lines to make sentences.

1 We

was	playing	cards	at 2 o'clock yesterday.
are	watching	TV	at 5 o'clock yesterday.
were	making	with toys	at 7 o'clock yesterday.

2 What

was	you	did	in here this morning?
is	your	do	in here tomorrow?
were	yours	doing	in here next Tuesday?

3 Was

she	flying	the piano	at 8 o'clock?
they	doing	a kite	at 9 o'clock?
he	playing	his homework	at 10 o'clock?

4 I

was	watch	TV on	3 o'clock.
were	watched	TV at	4 o'clock.
is	watching	TV in	5 o'clock.

4 Two return tickets

1 Match and write the words.

plat	driver
ticket	of tea
train	lator
esca	case
a cup of	airs
a cup	form
ruck	tion
st	coffee
suit	sack
sta	office

1 _____

2 platform

3 _____

4 _____

5 _____

6 _____

7 _____

8 _____

9 _____

10 _____

2 Read and write the words.

1 This is a popular drink. You make it from beans. _coffee_

2 Trains leave from and arrive at it. _____

3 You carry your things in it. You carry it on your back. _____

4 You walk up or down them. _____

5 You carry your things in it. You move it with your hand. _____

6 It takes you up or down. _____

7 You buy your ticket here. _____

8 You wait here for the train to arrive. _____

ZZZ

1 Read and circle.

1 The train leaves **at** / **on** six.

2 Dinner is **on** / **at** eight.

3 I'm going to ride my bike **in** / **on** the afternoon.

4 The volleyball match is **at** / **on** Saturday.

5 It was very hot **in** / **on** April.

6 We sometimes watch TV **at** / **in** the evening.

2 Write *at*, *in* or *on*.

1 _on_ Monday

2 ___ 11 o'clock

3 ___ February

4 ___ Saturday

5 ___ the evening

6 ___ the morning

7 ___ your birthday

8 ___ dinnertime

9 ___ March

10 ___ 2014

11 ___ 6 o'clock

12 ___ 2008

3 Write sentences about yourself.

When do you …

1 … do your homework?

I do my homework in the evening.

2 … watch TV?

_____

3 … go to bed?

_____

4 … have lunch?

_____

5 … relax?

_____

6 What month is your birthday?

_____

1 **Remember the song. Correct the sentences.**

1 On Monday at five he sails his big canoe.

   On Monday at three he climbs the apple tree.

2 On Tuesday at three he plays football.

_____

3 On Wednesday at six he does sports in the sports centre.

_____

4 On Thursday at two he flies his kite.

_____

5 On Friday at four he watches TV.

_____

6 On Saturday and Sunday he takes his dog for a walk.

_____

2 **Look at the pictures. Complete the poem.**

Monday

There was an old lady called Knocks.
On Monday she fed her pet (1) *fox*_____ .
On Tuesday at (2)_____
She always (3)_____ **tea**
And she sat in a big cardboard (4)_____ .

Tuesday

On Wednesday she mended the (5)_____
And on Thursday she cleaned all the (6)_____ .
On (7)_____ **at four**
She painted the (8)_____ .
That funny old lady called Knocks!

Wednesday

Thursday

Friday

3 CD2 22 **Listen and check. Say the poem.**

1 Write *was* or *were*.

When the train arrived …

1 … I _was_ eating a sandwich,

2 … John and Peter _____ waiting on the platform,

3 … a man _____ reading a newspaper,

4 … two men _____ talking,

5 … a girl _____ sitting on her suitcase

6 … and a boy _____ buying a ticket.

2 Write sentences. Use the words from the box.

> sit / garden   build / tree house   ride / bike   play / volleyball

When it started to rain …

1 … _they were playing volleyball._

2 … _____ .

3 … _____ .

4 … _____ .

3 Write the verbs to complete the sentences.

1 Dad _was working_ in the garden when he _hurt_ his leg. (work / hurt)

2 I _____ my homework when you _____ me. (do / phone)

3 When I _____ the party, my friends _____ . (leave / dance)

4 I _____ to music when Mum _____ me. (listen / call)

1 Remember the story. Complete the sentences.

1 At Broom station, Lucy and Ben _see Horax and Zelda_ .
2 Ben tells Lucy to _____ .
3 Zelda and Horax want to _____ .
4 Ben can see that the train is _____ .
5 When the conductor comes, Horax can't _____ .
6 Horax and Zelda must _____ .

2 Write sentences. Use the words from the box.

Lucy's   ~~Ben's~~   Horax's   Ben and Lucy's   Horax and Zelda's

1 _This is Ben's dog._

2 _____

3 _____

4 _____

5 _____

3 What happened in the tunnel? Complete the story. Use the verbs from the box and other words.

put   stood   took   ~~went~~

When they _went_ through _____ , Ben _____ up.
He _____ out of _____
and he _____ .

4

1 CD2 26 **Listen and write the missing words. Then say with a friend.**

1

Anna: When are we going to wrap Dad's present?

James: Well, he's working in the garden at the moment, look.

Anna: Great! _____ _____ !

2

Hannah: Hey, Joe. What's that?

Joe: What? Where?

Hannah: That. Can't you see?

_____ _____

_____ .

Joe: I can't see anything.

Hannah: Ah, it isn't there now.

Joe: Hey! My crisps!

2 **Look, read and write the words.**

chair   pear   stairs   wearing   hair   ~~bears~~

 1

 2

 3

 4

1 He's **scared** of the _bears_ .

2 **Clare** has got long _____ .

3 Please **share** the _____ .

4 **Where** are the _____ ?

5 He's _____ an old **pair** of trousers.

6 It's over **there** on that _____ .

 5

6

3 CD2 27 **Listen, say and check your answers.**

1 🎧 CD2 28 **Listen and tick (✓) the box.**

1 Who was on the platform?

A ✓   B ☐   C ☐

2 Who was on the train?

A ☐   B ☐   C ☐

3 What happened after the tunnel?

A ☐   B ☐   C ☐

4 What happened at the station?

A ☐   B ☐   C ☐

5 What did the old lady do?

A ☐   B ☐   C ☐

1 Read and write the correct prices.

1 L o n d o n	£7.80
2 C a m b r i d g e	
3 O x f o r d	
4 B r i s t o l	
5 N e w c a s t l e	
6 H u l l	

1 A: How much is a single ticket to London?
   B: It's seven pounds eighty.
   A: Here you are.
   B: Thanks, and there's your change.

2 A: How much is a single ticket to Cambridge?
   B: That's five pounds twenty.
   A: Here you are.
   B: Thanks. Here's your ticket.

3 A: A ticket to Oxford, please. How much is it?
   B: Single or return?
   A: Single.
   B: It's seven pounds sixty.
   A: Here you are.

4 A: How much is a single ticket to Bristol?
   B: It's twelve forty.
   A: Twelve fifty?
   B: No, it's twelve pounds forty.

5 A: A single to Newcastle, please. How much is it?
   B: Twenty-six pounds.
   A: Here you are.
   B: Thank you. Here's your change.

6 A: How much is a ticket to Hull?
   B: Single or return?
   A: Single.
   B: It's nineteen pounds seventy.

2 Write sentences with *o'clock*, *half past* or *quarter to / past*.

Cambridge
The train to Cambridge leaves at twelve o'clock.

Oxford
_____
_____
_____

Newcastle
_____
_____
_____

Bristol
_____
_____
_____

London
_____
_____

Hull
_____
_____

1 **Look and write the words.**

push ~~fall~~ drop smooth pull rough

1 _fall_

2 _____

3 _____

4 _____

5 _____

6 _____

2 **Values** **Read and tick (✓) the correct picture.**

When you lift a heavy box, you should always push up from the bottom. Don't pull the box up because it hurts your back.

Be careful when something is too high for you. Put a stepladder near the shelf. Stand on the stepladder and put your arms out, but keep your body straight. Don't lean away from the stepladder.

1 Read and write the words.

> rough   stop   faster   smooth   ~~go down~~

1 When you _go down_ a slide, gravity pulls you to the bottom.

2 There is also a force trying to _____ you. It is called friction.

3 If the surface of the slide is _____ , the friction is bigger.
You go more slowly.

4 If the surface of the slide is _____ , the friction is smaller.
You go _____ .

2 Think! Read and write 1, 2 or 3.

These children are going at the same speed on their bikes. Then they put on their brakes. Look at the surface where they are riding. Which bike is going to stop first? Number the pictures 1 (the first) to 3 (the last).

a

b

c

1 CD2 30 **Put the dialogue in order. Then listen and check.**

☐ **A:** To London. OK. When do you want to leave?

☐ **B:** Here you are.

☐ **A:** Single or return?

☐ **B:** Half past eight is fine. How much is the ticket?

1 **A:** Hello. How can I help you?

☐ **B:** Thank you. Oh, and what platform number is it, please?

☐ **A:** The return ticket is £42.

☐ **B:** Return, please.

☐ **A:** Thanks. And here's your change.

☐ **B:** I want to go to London, please.

☐ **A:** Platform 2.

☐ **B:** In the morning.

☐ **A:** There's a train at seven and one at half past eight.

2 **Look and write a dialogue. Use language from Activity 1.**

Cambridge
Single
???

£15.20
platform 3

Hello. Can I help you?

1 Think! Which one is different in each group? Look, think and circle.

2 Colour the bricks to make sentences. Write in the missing words.

1	When the train	_____ TV when	Saturday.
2	My birthday party	arrived, Dad was	you phoned me.
3	I was	holiday _____	August for two weeks.
4	We're going on	too fast	when he _____ an accident.
5	Paul was driving	is _____	buying a _cup_ of coffee.

5 Police!

1 Look, read and number the sentences.

①   ②   ③

a ☐ He's got long dark hair. It's straight.

b ☐ He's got fair curly hair. He's got a beard and a moustache.

c ☐ He's got short blonde hair. He's got a scar below his mouth.

2 Read and draw Danni's face.

WANTED
Dangerous Danni

She's got long hair. It's black. She's got a long scar on her face and a small scar between her eyes. She's very dangerous.

DON'T speak to her. Call the police!

3 Write and draw a *Wanted* poster.

WANTED

_____

_____

_____

_____

1 Look at the pictures. Read and write *t* (true) or *f* (false).

1980   **Now**

1 Dad used to have long hair.   t
2 Dad used to have a scar.
3 Dad used to have a beard.
4 Dad used to have a moustache.
5 Dad used to have straight hair.
6 Dad used to have dark hair.

2 Complete the sentences. Use the words from the box.

cry sleep eat ~~drink~~ play crawl

When I was a baby …

1 I _used to drink_
milk.

2 I _____
a lot.

3 I _____
in a cot.

4 I _____
baby food.

5 I _____ on
my hands and knees.

6 I _____
with my teddy bear.

3 Write sentences about you.

When I was four …

1 _____
2 _____
3 _____

1 Remember the song. What did Dad use to look like?
Tick (✓) the correct pictures.

1 a □   b □   c □

2 a □   b □   c □

3 a □   b □   c □

2 Write four sentences about Mum.

Mum used to wear glasses.

_____

_____

_____

Mum before   **Mum now**

3 Read and write the words.

week   time   me   ~~hair~~   early   sing   curly   anything

I used to have beautiful (1) _hair_ .
It was blonde and (2) _____ .
Now I dye it black each (3) _____
Because it went grey so (4) _____ !

I used to wear glasses all the (5) _____ .
I couldn't see (6) _____ .
The doctor fixed my eyes for (7) _____ —
It made me want to (8) _____ !

4 Listen and check. Say the poem.

1 **Read and write the words.**

wear   help   ~~arrive~~   do   learn

When I was a schoolboy …

1   … I had to _arrive_ at school before 7 o'clock.

2   … I had to _____ a uniform.

3   … I had to _____ French, German and Spanish.

4   … I had to _____ homework for two hours every night.

5   … I had to _____ the teacher with the younger students.

2 **Write sentences.**

When I lived at home, I had to work hard every day.

1   I had to tidy up.

2   _____

3   _____

4   _____

5   _____

6   _____

Now I live in my own house, I don't have to do things every day!

1 Remember the story. Complete the sentences.

1 The Mysterious H stole from _jewellers_ in London.

2 He stole from museums all over the _____ .

3 The story of The Mysterious H was in all the _____ .

4 He even stole the top of the Eiffel _____ .

5 He always used to leave a _____ with an *H* on it.

6 The _____ in the restaurant was wearing a ring with an *H* on it.

2 Remember The Mysterious H's rhyme. Write the words in order.

but / find / anywhere / here / you / look / look / there / ~~you~~ / you / can't / me

You _____ . _____ .

_____ .

3 Where did The Mysterious H steal these things from? Draw lines and write sentences.

a museum

the castle

a jeweller's shop

an art gallery

Paris

1 _He stole the painting from an art gallery._

2 _____

3 _____

4 _____

5 _____

1 CD2 41 Listen and write the missing words. Then say with a friend.

Abby: You're famous.

Chris: I'm sorry, what did you say?

Abby: You're famous. Look.

_____ _____

_____ _____

_____ .

Chris: Oh no! I must change my hair again.

Jeremy: Oh no! It got away!

Lionel: Again? You're just not lucky today!

Jeremy: _____ _____

_____ _____ .

Lionel: Maybe next time.

2 Look, read and number the sentences.

a ☐ They were walking in North Park when a terrible storm started.

b ☐1 Paul and Dawn went out at quarter past four in the morning.

c ☐ The rescue team saw the light and took Paul and Dawn to their car.

d ☐ They couldn't find their car in the dark, so Dawn used her torch.

3 CD2 42 Listen, say and check your answers.

1 (Values) What can we learn from the story? Colour the words.

Find Don't make take her

other people's things words .

2 Look and write the words.

my enemy   a seed   ~~a piece of apple~~
a shoulder   a farmer   a juicy orange

1 _a piece of apple_

2 _____

3 _____

4 _____

5 _____

6 _____

3 (Think!) Put the story in order.

[ ] The police officer tells the farmer that Yatin is sorry.
[1] Yatin eats an orange from the tree.
[ ] Yatin goes home.
[ ] Yatin thinks about his mum and dad.
[ ] The farmer catches Yatin.
[ ] The farmer gives Yatin a bag of seeds.
[ ] The farmer goes to fetch the police officer.
[ ] Yatin works for the farmer.

1 Look at the pictures. Write the story.

One day a boy was in a shop.

1 Correct the sentences.

1 Agatha Christie is only popular in the UK.

   No, she's popular all over the world.

2 She disappeared in the 1930s for 20 days.

_____

3 Conan Doyle was 81 when he died.

_____

4 He also wrote love stories.

_____

5 Miss Marple appeared in 11 novels.

_____

6 Sherlock Holmes' friend was called Mr Watson.

_____

7 Sherlock Holmes used to play the piano.

_____

8 Hercule Poirot was from France.

_____

2 Read and write the name from Activity 1.

_____

has got fair hair, but he hasn't got a lot of hair. It's straight. He's got a fair moustache.

 A

 B

3 Write a description of photo B.

_____

_____

_____

4 Write A and B.

Photo _____ is a detective from a book. Photo _____ is a real writer.

1 **Remember the story. Number the pictures.**

a [ ]

b [1]

c [ ]

d [ ]

e [ ]

2 **Write two cases for Sherlock Holmes. Use ideas from the box or your own ideas.**

> in a castle   on a farm   in a big city   on a boat
> a young woman   an old man   a doctor
> a missing dog   a missing bracelet   a missing child   a missing painting
> a book in code   an old newspaper   a mysterious letter

1   The story takes place _____ .

Sherlock Holmes helps _____ to find _____ .

He has to read _____ to solve the case.

2   The story takes place _____ .

Holmes and Watson _____

_____

_____

_____

1 Match the questions with the answers.

1 Where do you like to read?

2 How many books do you read a week?

3 What are your favourite kind of books?

4 Do you like love stories?

5 What kind of things do you read?

6 What's best, watching TV or reading?

a ☐ Reading, definitely, but I like TV.

b ☐ I love crime stories.

c ☐ 1 ☐ The best place is in bed!

d ☐ About two.

e ☐ No, I don't. I never read them.

f ☐ I read comics and I sometimes read my dad's newspaper.

2 Look at Activity 1. <u>Underline</u> the mistakes. Then write the correct sentences.

Lucy <u>likes reading, but she loves</u> watching TV too. Her favourite place to read is on the sofa. She reads more than three books a week. Her favourite kind of books are science fiction stories. She never reads historical novels. As well as reading books, she reads comics and magazines.

Lucy loves reading, but she likes watching TV too.

_____

_____

_____

_____

_____

3 Write about your reading habits.

I like reading in bed.

1 Write the words in four groups.

> ~~beard~~ ~~blonde~~ ~~curly~~ dark ~~farmer~~ light
> moustache orange scar seed short straight

1
beard

2
blonde

3
curly

4
farmer

2 Look at Activity 1. Number the topics to match the groups.

☐ Hair colour   ☐ Face   ☐ Story words   ☐ Hair style

3 Look and draw lines to make sentences.

1 Mum's family

used to	living	in France	in the 1980s.
used	lived	by France	at the 1980s.
use to	live	on France	on the 1980s.

2 I

had to	tidying	my bedroom	yesterday.
have to	tidied	the kitchen	tomorrow.
has to	tidy	the living room	now.

3 My mum

used	being	an actress	when she was born.
was	be	a teacher	before I was born.
used to	been	a doctor	before she was born.

4 My dad

had	help	my dad	in the shop.
had to	helped	his dad	in the cinema.
have to	helping	our dad	at the zoo.

⑥ Mythical beasts

① Look and complete the words.

1 h o r n

2 _ _ o _ g _

3 _ _ _ c _ _

4 _ _ a t _ _ _ s

5 _ _ _ _ _ g

6 _ _ _ c _

7 t _ _ _ _ _

8 _ _ _ a _ _ s

② Look, read and number the texts.

a [ ]   This dragon has got wings. The feathers on the wings are beautiful.
They've got grey and white patterns. The dragon's neck is long and it's got
scales. There are also scales on its back and there are feathers on its back
too. It's got a short tail, a long tongue and two horns.

b [ ]   This dragon has got wings. The grey feathers on the wings are beautiful.
The dragon has got scales on its back and also on its long neck.
It's got a long tongue, a horn and a short tail.

c [ ]   This dragon has got wings. The feathers on the wings are beautiful
and you can see black and white patterns on them. It's got a long neck,
a short tail, two horns and a long tongue. It's got feathers on its back
and scales on its neck.

③ Write about the other dragon from Activity 2.

_____

_____

_____

① Read and write *t* (true) or *f* (false).

1 The world's longest snake

The python holds the world record for the longest snake. The record-breaker was 9.92 m! The python is longer than the anaconda, but anacondas are the world's fattest snakes.

3 The world's worst singer

The 'crex-crex' song of the corncrake sounds so terrible that this bird is certainly the world's worst singer.

2 More aggressive than you think

It looks friendly in cartoons, but the hippo is probably the most dangerous land animal in Africa. (Maybe the mosquito is even more dangerous?) Hippos are very aggressive, not scared of humans and much more dangerous than lions.

4 Crocodiles – the smallest and the heaviest

The smallest crocodile is the dwarf crocodile of West Africa, which hardly ever grows bigger than 1.5 m long. The heaviest crocodiles are saltwater crocodiles, which can grow to 7 m long and weigh over 1,000 kg!

1 Pythons are the longest snakes, but anacondas can be fatter.   `t`

2 The longest snake was more than 10 m.   ☐

3 Hippos are very dangerous, but they run from humans.   ☐

4 The song of the corncrake isn't very nice at all.   ☐

5 Saltwater crocodiles aren't longer than dwarf crocodiles.   ☐

② Write sentences.

1 Anacondas / fat / snakes in the world

  Anacondas are the fattest snakes in the world.

2 Hippos / dangerous / lions

_____

3 Corncrakes / bad / singers in the world

_____

4 Dwarf crocodiles / small / saltwater crocodiles

_____

1 Remember the song. Correct the sentences.

1 In my dream I met the most dangerous dragon.

In my dream I met the most beautiful dinosaur.

2 Its head was smaller than a tractor.

_____

3 Its neck was longer than a tower.

_____

4 Its scales were stronger than wood.

_____

5 Its eyes were bigger than me.

_____

6 It had the best teeth on Earth.

_____

2 Write adjectives to complete the sentences.

In my dream I met (1) the most dangerous dinosaur. (dangerous)

Its teeth were (2) _____ _____ knives. (sharp)

Its wings were (3) _____ _____ planes. (long)

It was (4) _____ _____ animal on land. (strong)

It was (5) _____ _____ runner and

(6) _____ _____ at flying. (fast / good)

3 Imagine a dragon or a dinosaur. Draw and write about it.

1 **Write questions for the answers. Use the words from the box.**

> Pegasus   the Sphinx   a mermaid   a unicorn   the Phoenix   ~~a centaur~~

1 *What does a centaur look like?* — It's half horse and half man.

2 _____ — She's got the head of a woman and the tail of a fish.

3 _____ — It's a bird with very big wings and red and golden feathers.

4 _____ — It looks like a horse, but it's got wings and can fly.

5 _____ — It's a white horse with a long horn in the middle of its head.

6 _____ — It looks like a lion with a human head.

2 **Think!** **Read the dialogue. Write 1, 2, 3 or 4.**

A: What does Cloud ____ look like?

B: I think it looks like a dog. It's driving a car.

Write dialogues about the other pictures.

A: _____

B: _____

A: _____

B: _____

A: _____

B: _____

1 **Remember the story. Put the sentences in order.**

- [ ] The children find a way out, but they have to jump into the pool.
- [1] Lucy finds a door in the dragon.
- [ ] Horax and Zelda see Ben and Lucy, but the children run away.
- [ ] On the side of the pool, they find the next line for the rhyme.
- [ ] The children open it and go in.
- [ ] It's a trap! Horax closes the door and they can't get out.

2 Think! **Read and circle.**

1 Picture 1: Why is Ben standing in front of the dragon?

  A Because he hopes to see a smile on the dragon's face.

  B Because he hopes he can jump in the pool.

  C Because he hopes to see the next line on the dragon's tongue.

2 Picture 6: Why do the children jump into the pool?

  A Because it's the only way to get out.

  B Because it's a very hot day.

  C Because Horax and Zelda can't swim.

3 Picture 7: Why does Lucy say 'Hurry up!'?

  A Because they are wet and cold and want to go home.

  B Because she thinks Horax and Zelda can catch them.

  C Because school starts in fifteen minutes.

3 Think! **Complete Horax's diary entry.**

Today was a (1) _bad_ day for Zelda and me. We saw (2) _____ .
They were looking at (3) _____ . We were
sure the next line (4) _____
but then they opened (5) _____ and
(6) _____ . Zelda and I (7) _____ .
In the end the children (8) _____ and they
(9) _____ . Zelda and I were very (10) _____ .

1 CD 3 12 **Listen and write the missing words. Then say with a friend.**

1

2

Ollie: I don't believe it. The ball's really high up in the tree.

Jem: And that tree's too dangerous to climb.

Ollie: We could get my dad's ladder.

Jem: Yes. _____ _____

_____ _____ .

Mum: Where are you?

Dad: He's here somewhere.

Connor: Hee, hee, hee.

Mum: _____ _____

_____ _____

_____ .

Connor: Hee, hee, hee.

Mum and Dad: There you are!

Connor: Ha!

2 **Complete the table with the words from the box.**

~~weather~~ eat team feather beans bread head meat

beast	treasure
_____	weather
_____	_____
_____	_____

3 CD 3 13 **Listen, say and check your answers.**

1 Remember Paul's dinosaur book in the Student's Book.
Read and write the words.

a castle   vegetables   ~~a cellar~~   mice   trees

Paul has got a great book about dinosaurs. He found
it in (1) _a cellar_ . The dinosaurs lived in (2) _____ .
They didn't like eating animals, so they didn't eat
(3) _____ , but they didn't eat (4) _____ either.
They loved eating (5) _____ from the garden.

2 Make sentences.

1   found / two / book / weeks / I / a / ago / unicorn / about / a
Two weeks ago I found a book about a unicorn.

2   the / book / the / was / of / name / *Unicornia*
_____

3   lived / forest / a fantastic / the / unicorn / in
_____

4   lots / trees / colourful / were / of / there
_____

5   unicorn / the / plants / eat / grass or / didn't
_____

6   only / eat / trees / wanted to / it / purple
_____

7   liked / book / the / I / very much / because / it / really interesting / was
_____

3 Imagine that you found a book about a mythical beast.
Write about it. Think about:

- What's the name of the book?
- Where did you find it?
- Where did the beast live?

- What did / didn't it eat?
- What did it love doing?
- Why did / didn't you like the book?

A week ago I found a book about

1 **Read and write *yes* or *no*.**

1   There are feathers on the dinosaur's wings.   *yes*

2   The unicorn is eating grass.

3   A big grey dragon is eating apples from a tree.

4   There are some flowers below the apple tree.

5   The snake with the horn is fatter than the other snake.

6   There is a chicken in the bigger snake's mouth.

7   There are lots of stones in the river.

8   It's sunny, but there are lots of clouds in the sky.

1 **Look and write the words.**

snakes   seals   spiders   moths   eagles   fish   lions   ~~antelopes~~

1 antelopes

2

3

4

5

6

7

8

2 **Write the animals from Activity 1 in two groups. Can any of the animals be in both groups?**

predators	prey
	antelopes

3 **Write about three more animals.**

Mice are predators. They eat moths and other insects.
Mice are also the prey of animals like cats and owls.

1 Read and write *predators* or *prey*.

All animals, (1) _predators_ and (2) _____ , must eat. Some animals eat only plants, others need plants and meat and some eat only meat. Animals that eat meat are called (3) _____ . The animals that (4) _____ eat are called (5) _____ . Animals that are (6) _____ have different ways to protect themselves against their (7) _____ . They use poison and weapons to fight (8) _____ , their speed to run away from them or their looks to confuse or scare the (9) _____ .

2 (Values) Read the dialogue. What can we learn from it? Tick (✓).

Harry: Nature's horrible.

Mia: Why do you say that? Just look how beautiful everything is: those birds, the butterflies, the flowers …

Harry: Yes, they're beautiful, but why do some animals eat other animals? Lions eat zebras, snakes eat mice and sharks eat smaller fish. It's terrible.

Mia: Yes, but it isn't because they're bad. They need to eat meat.

Harry: What do you mean? Can't they just eat plants?

Mia: Well, some animals eat plants only, others eat both plants and meat and others eat meat only. They need meat to survive.

Harry: You mean they can't live without eating meat?

Mia: Exactly. Lions can't live without meat. They die.

Harry: Hmm, I think I'm beginning to understand.

Mia: Understand what?

Harry: All animals are important. Lions need meat, so they need to hunt antelopes, zebras and other animals. When there aren't enough of them, lions can't eat.

Mia: That's right. And that's how animals die out.

- [ ] Some animals are good and some animals are bad. The bad ones are meat-eaters.
- [ ] We need to protect nature. Animals mustn't die out.
- [ ] Some animals are going to die out, but it doesn't matter. Nature has got enough animals.

1 CD3 15 **Put the dialogue in order. Then listen and check.**

[ ] **B:** What's strange about a white horse?

[ ] **A:** In the garden behind our house, 23 Queen's Park. It's eating all the flowers.

[ ] **B:** Really? What does it look like?

[1] **A:** Good afternoon. Can I speak to the director of the zoo, please?

[ ] **B:** OK. Try not to scare it. I'm coming to your house right now.

[ ] **A:** Well, it looks like a horse, a white horse.

[ ] **B:** That's me. How can I help you?

[ ] **A:** It's got a horn.

[ ] **B:** A white horse with a horn. Then it's a unicorn. Where did you find it?

[ ] **A:** I've got a strange animal. I found it this morning.

2 **Look and write a dialogue. Use language from Activity 1.**

I've got a strange animal. I found it this afternoon.

_____

_____

_____

_____

_____

_____

_____

1 **Which one is different in each group? Look, think and circle.**

2 **Colour the bricks to make sentences. Write in the missing words.**

1	What does	best sister _____	_____ ?
2	You're the	your sister	my mum.
3	What do	mermaids look	_____ the world!
4	That's the ugliest	is taller _____	the world!
5	My aunt	dog	_look_ like?

1 CD 3
8
18 **Listen and circle.**

1 recorder / (violin)

2 trombone / trumpet

3 drums / keyboard

4 keyboard / tambourine

5 trumpet / saxophone

6 violin / harp

7 triangle / drums

8 saxophone / trombone

9 tambourine / triangle

2 **Find the triangles and write sentences.**

There's a triangle under the tambourine.

1 Read and write the words.

hers   theirs   his   yours   ~~mine~~   ours

1 Is this your bike, Ken?
Yes, it's _mine_ .

2 Is this Peter's guitar?
Yes, it's _____ .

3 This isn't my pen. Take it.
It's _____ .

4 That's a nice scooter. Is it Jane's?
Yes, it's _____ .

5 Is this where you and Lily live?
Yes, this house is _____ .

6 This is Peter and Tom's car.
Is it really _____ ?

2 Change the sentences.

1 It's my dog. → It's _mine_ .

2 It's Mia's cat. → It's _____ .

3 They are John and Lucy's horses. → They're _____ .

4 This house is Ruby's and mine. → It's _____ .

5 It's John's violin. → It's _____ .

6 It's not my cap. It's your cap. → It's _____ .

3 Look and write sentences.

It's mine.

1 Remember the song. Tick (✓) or cross (✗) and write sentences.

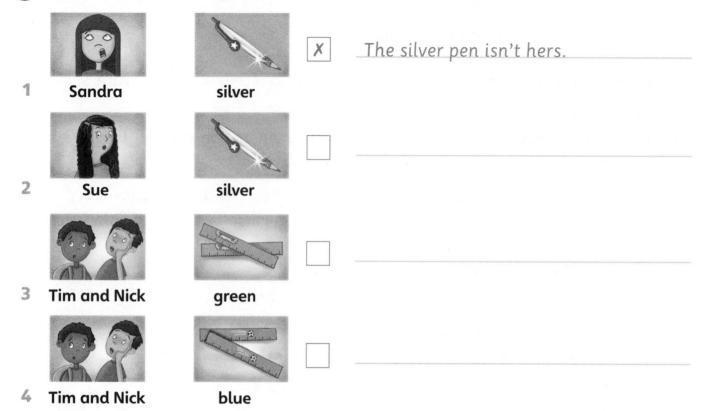

1 Sandra — silver ✗ *The silver pen isn't hers.*

2 Sue — silver ☐

3 Tim and Nick — green ☐

4 Tim and Nick — blue ☐

2 Follow the lines. Answer the questions.

Olivia Harry Luke Mia George and Ella Daisy and Jack

1 Is the cat George and Ella's? *No, it isn't theirs. It's Daisy and Jack's.*
2 Is the pencil case Mia's?
3 Is the book Harry's?
4 Is the dog Daisy and Jack's?
5 Is the pencil Olivia's?
6 Is the rucksack Luke's?

1 Read and circle.

1 Matt is the boy **who** / **which** plays the guitar.

2 Mexico is the country **which** / **where** my cousins live.

3 The house **who** / **which** you can see over there is Bob's.

4 Claire is the girl **where** / **who** is a very good footballer.

5 The instrument **which** / **who** George plays is the saxophone.

6 London is the city **who** / **where** I'd like to live.

2 Read and write *who*, *which* or *where*.

1 Max is the boy ___who___ reads lots of books.

2 The instrument _____ my friend plays is the violin.

3 The town _____ my grandparents live is near the coast.

4 Maria is the girl _____ likes listening to music.

5 The pen _____ is on the floor is Will's.

6 The farm _____ we ride horses is in the mountains.

3 Look and write four more sentences with *who* or *which*.

The boy who is reading is Jack.

The saxophone which is next to the sofa is Jack's.

_____

_____

_____

_____

1 **Remember the story. Read and write the words.**

apple   hides   banana   ~~café~~   takes   cup   line   open   starts   to

Lucy and Ben go to the (1) _café_ for a drink. They order orange juice, an (2) _____ , hot chocolate and a (3) _____ . Then Ben sees the (4) _____ on Lucy's (5) _____ . When the children are having their drinks, Horax looks in Ben's rucksack and he (6) _____ out the map. The conductor sees Horax and wants him (7) _____ leave. Horax (8) _____ the map in the trumpet. When Ben and Lucy come back, they see that Ben's rucksack is (9) _____ . When the trumpet player (10) _____ , the children find the map.

2 (Think!) **Read and write *t* (true) or *f* (false).**

1 Pictures 1 and 2: The children know that the line is in the café. | *f* |

2 Picture 4: Lucy can't read the line. | |

3 Picture 5: When Horax says, 'Very nice of you, kids. Thank you', he is talking to Ben and Lucy. | |

4 Picture 6: When the conductor arrives, Horax thinks of a trick. | |

5 Picture 7: The children know that the map is in the trumpet. | |

6 Picture 8: The trick which Horax plays doesn't work. | |

3 **Look and answer the questions.**

1 Is this Ben's?

No, it isn't his.

It's the conductor's.

2 Is this Lucy's?

_____

_____

3 Is this Horax's?

_____

_____

4 Is this the conductor's?

_____

_____

1 CD 3 27 **Listen and write the missing words. Then say with a friend.**

1

Mum: Be careful with those plates, Tom. Maybe you should only take two at a time?

Tom: Don't worry, Mum. … Whoops!

Mum: Tom!

Tom: _____ _____

_____ , Mum. I really am.

2

Debs: Where's Frank?

George: I don't know. There are just too many people.

Debs: Hey, look. There he is. Over there. Frank! Frank!

George: Oh yes, there he is!

_____ _____ ,

Debs!

2 **Write the words from the box in the *shirt* or the *door*.**

> ~~world~~ floor bird work call thirsty orchestra keyboard
> horn curly sword her four first purple talk

world

3 CD 3 28 **Listen, say and check your answers.**

1 **Values** **What can we learn from the story? Colour the words.**

It's   They're   sometimes   bad

important   to   be   have

different   sad   from   his

your   friends   family   .

2 **Read and write the words.**

laughed   ~~fell off~~   silent   invite   beautiful   day

1 The bear saw a big bag that _fell off_ a car.
2 In the bag there was a _____ violin.
3 The bear played the violin all _____ .
4 One day the bear said to his friends, 'I'd like to _____ you to a concert.'
5 After the concert his friends were _____ .
6 The animals _____ because they didn't like his music.

3 **Look at the pictures. Write the story.**

One day the elephant saw a trumpet.

1 Read the text. Choose the right words and write them on the lines.

Bears

There are eight different kinds of bears. Most bears ⁽¹⁾ _live_ in countries in the north, but the spectacled bear, which looks like a bear with glasses, lives in South America. There aren't any bears in Africa and Australia. There ⁽²⁾ _____ bears in northern Africa, but there aren't any there now.

Bears have a big body, strong teeth and a short tail. Most bears eat animals and plants, ⁽³⁾ _____ the polar bear only eats other animals and the panda only eats plants.

Baby bears and young bears stay ⁽⁴⁾ _____ their mothers, but when they are older they live alone.

Bears usually look ⁽⁵⁾ _____ food during the day, but sometimes they are out at night.

They can smell other animals and people from far away, they can ⁽⁶⁾ _____ very quickly, they can climb trees and they are also good swimmers.

In autumn most bears eat a lot and then they go to a cave to sleep in winter.

1	living	live	lives		4	at	up	with
2	were	was	is		5	on	in	for
3	but	so	because		6	runs	run	running

1 Look at the pictures. Read and write *t* (true) or *f* (false).

1 The bang in **a** is louder than in **b**.	*f*
2 The bang in **b** is louder than in **c**.	
3 The bang in **c** is louder than in **b**.	
4 The bang in **b** is louder than in **a**.	
5 The bang in **b** is the loudest.	

2 Look at the pictures. Complete the sentences.
Use the words from the box once or more times.

> higher   highest   lower   lowest   than   the

1 The sound in **a** is _lower_ _than_ the sound in **b**.
2 The sound in **b** is _____ _____ the sound in **c**.
3 The sound in **c** is _____ _____ the sound in **b**.
4 The sound in **b** is _____ _____ the sound in **a**.
5 The sound in **c** is _____ _____ .
6 The sound in **a** is _____ _____ .

1 Draw lines to match the opposites.

HIGH

LOUD

SHORT

LONG

QUIET

LOW

2 What sound do these instruments make?
Number the photos 1 (the lowest) to 3 (the highest).

1 (a)   (b)   (c)   [1]

2 (a)   (b)   (c)

3 (a)   (b)   (c)

1 **Match the questions with the answers.**

1 Do you play an instrument, Lily?

2 Would you like to play an instrument?

3 Who's your favourite singer?

4 Justin Bieber? Is he from the USA?

5 And what's your favourite song?

6 Is there a song which you really don't like?

a ☐ It's Justin Bieber.

b ☐ My favourite song? It's probably 'Never say never'.

c ☐ Yes, I'd like to play the violin.

d ☐ No, not by Justin! But I really don't like 'Someone like you' by Adele.

e ☐ 1 ☐ No, I don't.

f ☐ No, he's from Canada.

2 **Look at Activity 1. Underline the mistakes. Then write the correct sentences.**

Lily plays the guitar. She wouldn't like to play the violin. Her favourite singer is Justin Bieber. He is from America. Her favourite song is 'Never say never'. There is one song which she really doesn't like. It's called 'Someone like me'. It's by Usher.

Lily doesn't play an instrument.

_____

_____

_____

3 **Write about yourself and music.**

I play the piano and I'd like to play ...

1 Write the words in four groups.

~~drum~~ ~~guitar~~ harp ~~high~~ low loud ~~saxophone~~
tambourine triangle trombone trumpet violin

1 drum

2 guitar

3 high

4 saxophone

2 Look at Activity 1. Number the topics to match the groups.

☐ Stringed instruments   ☐ Sound words

☐ Wind instruments   ☐ Percussion instruments

3 Look and draw lines to make sentences.

1 It

isn't you	cap.	They're	my.
isn't your	caps.	He's	me.
isn't yours	book.	It's	mine.

2 The recorders

which	are on	the sofa	are us.
who	are next to	the chair	are ours.
where	are under	the cupboard	are violins.

3 I

thinks	this ball	were	hers.
think	these balls	are	yours.
thinking	those balls	is	theirs.

4 The girl

who is	sitting	opposite the tree	is my sister.
where is	sits	next to the tree	is hers.
which is	sit	on the tree	is my brother.

8 In the planetarium

1 **Read the sentences. Do the puzzle. Find the secret word.**

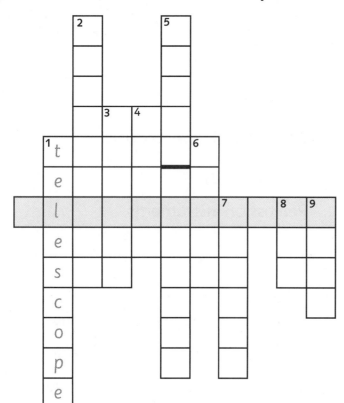

1 This is something which you use to look at the night sky.

2 He or she flies in a rocket.

3 Earth is one of these.

4 This has got a tail and it flies through the sky.

5 People stay and work here in space.

6 The night sky is full of these.

7 You use this to fly to the moon.

8 This is an alien spaceship.

9 Earth has got one of these.

2 **Look at Activity 1. Number the pictures.**

1 Follow the lines. Write the names and the sentences.

Elena	: I'll be a	n u r s e .
_____	:	t _ _ c h _ r .
_____	:	f _ r _ f _ ght _ r .
_____	:	c _ n d _ ct _ r .
_____	:	p _ l _ c _ _ ff _ c _ r .

2 Write five sentences about yourself.

When I grow up, I'll be an explorer. _____

I'll look for treasure. _____

I'll have lots of fun. _____

I'll travel the world. _____

I'll be very happy. _____

1 **Remember the song. Correct the sentences.**

1 The astronaut will build a space station.

   No, she'll live in a space station.

2 She'll fly to the sun in a rocket.

3 She'll ride on a comet and paint its tail.

4 She'll meet some aliens on the moon.

5 She'll visit some of the stars.

2 **What will you do when you're an astronaut? Write sentences.**

tidy up   build   fly   ~~fix~~

1 I'll fix my rocket.

2

3

4

3 **Imagine you meet aliens on Earth. Write four sentences.**

I'll show them my house.   I'll take them to the cinema.

1 **Write adverbs to complete the sentences.**

1 John is a good footballer, but yesterday he played __badly__ . (bad)

2 She sang the song _____ at the concert. (beautiful)

3 Uncle Rob is too fast on the road. He drives _____ . (dangerous)

4 When he saw the big dog, he ran back to his car _____ . (quick)

5 She loved her new toy and played _____ with it all day. (happy)

6 He didn't want to wake his brother so he spoke _____ . (quiet)

2 **Write sentences. Make adverbs with the adjectives from the box.**

> bad   dangerous   beautiful   ~~careful~~   quiet   loud

1 He _'s working carefully._

2 They _____ .

3 She _____ .

4 He _____ .

5 She _____ .

6 They _____ .

1 (Think!) **Remember the story. Put the sentences in order.**

☐ Zelda finds a poem.

☐ Lucy and Ben close the door.

☐ Ben's grandpa and a police officer arrive.

1 Lucy and Ben can't find the clue anywhere and they go for a drink.

☐ The police officer takes Horax and Zelda away.

☐ Horax and Zelda climb inside the rocket.

2 (Values) **Read the story. What can we learn from it? Tick (✓).**

'Can we have fish for dinner, please?' Gan and his younger brother Li
asked their mother. 'No, I'm sorry. Fish is too expensive,' she answered,
'but Gan, you can try to catch some in the lake.'

   'I'll go too,' said Li.

   'No,' said Gan quickly, 'I'll bring enough fish for all of us.'

   Gan went to the lake. He saw an old man fishing, but Gan didn't speak to him.
He put some bread on the hook and started fishing. After two hours,
he didn't have any fish and he decided to go home. On his way,
he saw that the old man had five fish and Gan was angry.

   The next day, Li asked Gan, 'Are you going fishing today?'

   'There aren't any fish there,' Gan answered and he went out to play.

   Li took the fishing rod and went to the lake. The old man was there again.

   'Hello,' said Li, 'can I sit next to you?'

   'Yes, of course,' the old man answered.

   When Li put some bread on the hook, the old man said, 'The fish in this lake
don't like bread, so I'll give you some corn.'

   After two hours, Li had five fish. 'Thank you very much,' he said to the old man.
The old man smiled.

☐ Older people don't know anything.

☐ Older people should be friendly when they meet young people.

☐ Older people can teach us things.

1 Listen and write the missing words. Then say with a friend.

1

Carl: Look at the ball!
Millie: We did it!
Carl: Yes. _____ _____
_____ _____ .
Millie: I'll be an astronaut one day!

2

Ryan: I've no idea how to get there.
Beth: Yes, it's a bit confusing but
_____ _____ _____ _____ .
Ryan: OK. First we need to find where we are.
Beth: Yes, and then we can see where we need to go.

2 Look and write the words.

farmer driver taller smaller clever river ~~teacher~~ waiter

1 teacher 2 _____ 3 _____ 4 _____

5 _____ 6 _____ 7 _____ 8 _____

3 Listen, say and check your answers.

1 **Read the text and choose the best answer. Lucas is talking to an alien.**

1 **Lucas:** Can you understand me?

   Alien: A ✓ Yes, I can.

            B ☐ Yes, I am.

            C ☐ Yes, I have.

2 **Lucas:** Where is your spaceship?

   Alien: A ☐ It's great.

            B ☐ It's behind the hill.

            C ☐ Here you are.

3 **Lucas:** When did you arrive?

   Alien: A ☐ Twelve o'clock is fine.

            B ☐ In front of the house.

            C ☐ An hour ago.

4 **Lucas:** Would you like to come to my house?

   Alien: A ☐ I like your house a lot.

            B ☐ Yes, please. I'd like to see it.

            C ☐ Yes, please. My house is great.

5 **Lucas:** Are you hungry?

   Alien: A ☐ Yes, please.

            B ☐ Yes, it is.

            C ☐ Yes, I am.

6 **Alien:** Have you got any cheese?

   Lucas: A ☐ Yes, I have.

            B ☐ Yes, I like it.

            C ☐ Yes, it does.

1 Read the story. Number the pictures.

A hot day in the mountains

Last July my parents, my brother and I were on holiday in the mountains.

One day when Dad was driving on a mountain road, he suddenly stopped the car. 'Look!' he shouted. We all looked, but no-one could see anything. 'I saw an alien, I'm sure. It went over that hill.'

We all got out of the car and started to walk up the hill. When we got to the top, we all saw the alien walk behind some rocks. We ran to the rocks but when we got there, it wasn't there. We walked back to the road, but now our car wasn't there. We went to the nearest village and told our story to a police officer. When we finished, he told us that he had some good news. 'I think we've got your car,' he said. He took us to the back of the police station and there was our car. We were very happy. 'And the alien?' asked Dad. 'Do you believe us?'

'I think we've got your alien too. Come with me,' said the police officer. We went inside and in the police station we saw two men. One of them was wearing an alien costume. 'This is your alien,' said the police officer, 'and this is his friend. While you were following the alien, his friend took your car.'

2 Look at the pictures. Write the story.

One day we were walking ...

1 Write the names of the planets.

Mercury

V

J

N

Sun

E

M

S

U

2 Read the text on the solar system in the Student's Book again. Complete the sentences.

1 There are _eight_ planets in our solar system.

2 The name of the biggest star in our solar system is the _____ .

3 The distance through a planet or a star from one side to the other is the _____ .

4 When the planets go around the sun we say that they _____ the sun.

5 It takes Earth _____ days to orbit the sun.

6 The smaller things that orbit the planets are called _____ .

3 Make sentences.

1 The sun is in

2 A 'year' is the time it takes

3 The length of a year

4 The only star we can see

5 The sun is more than

6 Some planets have

a ☐ is different on all planets.

b ☐ a million times bigger than Earth.

c ☐ a lot of moons.

d ☐ 1 ☐ the middle of the solar system.

e ☐ during the day is the sun.

f ☐ a planet to orbit the sun.

1 **Read the text. Write questions for the answers.**

Saturn is a very big planet. It's about ten times bigger than Earth and it's about ten times further away from the sun than Earth. The gases that make Saturn are very, very cold, so the temperature is −180°C. It's much colder than anywhere on our planet and only Neptune is colder in our solar system. Saturn is famous for its thousands of beautiful rings, which are ice. We know a lot about Saturn because in 1979 a spacecraft, Pioneer 11, visited Saturn and took lots of photos. Saturn has got about 60 moons. This is more than any other planet.

1   How big is Saturn? _____   It's about ten times bigger than Earth.

2   _____ ?   It's −180°C.

3   _____ ?   No, it isn't. Neptune is the coldest planet.

4   _____ ?   They are ice.

5   _____ ?   It visited Saturn in 1979.

6   _____ ?   About 60.

2 **Read, draw and colour. Write the names of the three moons.**

This is my planet. It's called Solron. It's red because it's very hot, like a fire! Solron has got three moons. They are called Fe, Fi and Fo. Fo is the biggest and Fe is the smallest. The planet has also got two rings. Nobody lives on Solron because it's too hot.

1 CD 4 15 **Put the dialogue in order. Then listen and check.**

☐ **A:** Hi, Gog. Nice to meet you. How old are you?

☐ **B:** I'm collecting rocks. It's my hobby – intergalactic rock-collecting. What about you? Have you got a hobby?

1 **A:** Hello. Do you speak my language?

☐ **B:** I'm Gog.

☐ **A:** 45 languages! That's great. I'm Mary Franklin. What's your name?

☐ **B:** That would be great. I'd love to.

☐ **A:** I'm 12. Gog, tell me, what are you doing here on Earth?

☐ **B:** Yes, I do. I can understand you, Earth girl. I speak 45 languages.

☐ **A:** Yes, I collect badges. Would you like to see them?

☐ **B:** I'm 235 years old. How old are you, Mary?

2 **Look and write a dialogue. Use language from Activity 1.**

name?   age?

hobby?   languages?

Hello, Earth boy.

1 **Write the words in four groups.**

astronaut   comet   Earth   Mercury   moon   Neptune
rocket   Saturn   space station   star   Uranus   Venus

1
astronaut

2
comet

3
Earth

4
Neptune

2 **Look at Activity 1. Number the topics to match the groups.**

☐ Colder planets   ☐ Humans in space

☐ Hotter planets   ☐ The night sky

3 **Colour some of the stars to find a planet. Write the word under the puzzle.**

4 **Colour the bricks to make sentences. Write in the missing words and letters.**

1	He did	you be	so I couldn't hear her.
2	She spoke	the exercise	when you grow up?
3	I'll	the old	vase careful____ .
4	What ____	very quiet____ ,	one day.
5	Please clean	____ famous	very bad_ly_ .

1 **Draw lines to make holiday activities.**

1	sail	a	the water
2	row	b	wood
3	put up	c	a boat
4	collect	d	a rope
5	make	e	a boat
6	make	f	a fire
7	swing on	g	your clothes
8	dive into	h	a raft
9	dry	i	a tent

2 **Look and write sentences.**

Jamie

Freya

Paul

1 _He's sailing a boat._   2 _____   3 _____

Rebecca

Marco

Ruth

4 _____   5 _____   6 _____

Liam

Sophie

Matt

7 _____   8 _____   9 _____

1 Look and complete the phrases.

1 some _____ biscuits

2 _a packet of_ biscuits

3 _____ milk

4 _____ milk

5 _____ tomatoes

6 _____ tomatoes

7 _____ bread

8 _____ bread

2 Look and complete the dialogues.

1 **A:** Would you like _a packet of sweets_?
   B: Yes, please.

2 **A:** Let's take a _____
      to the party.
   B: That's a good idea.

3 **A:** Would you like _____
      on your pasta?
   B: No, thanks.

4 **A:** Can I have a _____,
      please?
   B: Yes, of course. Chocolate cake or fruit cake?

5 **A:** I'd like two _____,
      please.
   B: That's £1.90.

1 Remember the song. Number the food.

- [ ] a bottle of juice
- [ ] a packet of crisps
- [ ] a bar of chocolate
- [ ] a loaf of bread
- [1] a piece of cheese

2 What's missing? Write sentences.

1 *The piece of cheese is missing.*

2 _____

3 _____

4 _____

3 (Think!) What's the problem? Read and draw lines.

We're going on a picnic with our picnic basket.

| My little sister put | a can of fruit, | some ice cream | and some eggs | in our picnic basket ... |

but ...

so we didn't eat them!

1 Write *much* or *many*, *is* or *are*.

1 How <u>much</u> cheese <u>is</u> there?

2 How _____ eggs _____ there?

3 How _____ apples _____ there?

4 How _____ milk _____ there?

5 How _____ bread _____ there?

6 How _____ bottles of water _____ there?

2 Look at the picture. Answer the questions from Activity 1.

1 There are three pieces of cheese.

2 _____

3 _____

4 _____

5 _____

6 _____

3 What else is in the fridge? Write dialogues.

A: How much chocolate is there ?

B: There are four bars of chocolate.

A: _____ ?

B: _____

A: _____ ?

B: _____

A: _____ ?

B: _____

1 Remember the story. Make sentences.

1 The children find the last line

2 Then they put the rhyme

3 They go to the lighthouse

4 The key which they need is

5 Buster helps to find the chest

6 Horax and Zelda read about it

a ☐ in order.

b ☐ behind a picture.

c ☐ in a newspaper.

d ☐ under the floor.

e ☐ on the beach.

f 1 on an oar.

2 Complete Ben and Lucy's story. Use two words from the box in each sentence.

dragon   ring   conductor   accident   restaurant   rocket   door   map   car
train   treasure   ~~shield~~   trumpet   lighthouse   trap   man   ~~knight~~   tunnel

1 Lucy and Ben find the first line _on the knight's shield_ .

2 Horax tries to steal _____ .

3 Grandpa helps a man who has _____ .

4 When _____ , Ben takes the baddies' tickets.

5 Grandpa wanted to catch a _____ who had _____ with *H* on it.

6 Horax and Zelda _____ the children _____ .

7 When Horax sees _____ , he puts the map _____ .

8 Ben and Lucy play a trick and close _____ .

9 They find _____ .

3 Write the lines of the rhyme in order.

There's the key to end this game.

Climb more stairs and look out west.

In the lighthouse you will see

Behind the picture in the frame

Lots of stairs. Climb thirty-three!

Look down and find the treasure chest.

In the lighthouse you will see

1 CD4 26 **Listen and write the missing words. Then say with a friend.**

Mum: So, Esme, what do you think?

Esme: Well, erm, _____ _____ beautifully.

Mum: Yes, I know. But is it nice? Come on, tell me.

Esme: Erm, it's horrible, Mum.

Kate: OK, so where are we?

Chris: I'm not sure. But I think we're quite close now.

Kate: But _____ _____ do we have to go?

Chris: Erm, I don't know.

2 **Look and write the words once or more times.**

> *bottle   can   loaf   packet   piece   cup*

1 a _cup_ of **tea**

2 a _____ of **crisps**

3 a _____ of **bread**

4 a _____ of **cake**

5 a _____ of **lemonade**

6 a _____ of **chocolate**

7 a _____ of **peas**

8 a _____ of **biscuits**

9 a _____ of **water**

3 CD4 27 **Listen, say and check your answers.**

Functions; phonics focus **111**

1 (Values) **What can we learn from the story? Colour the words.**

| Don't | Do | tell | do |

| bad | happy | stories | things | to |

| from | animals | sea | . |

2 **Look at the pictures and the letters in the box. Write the words.**

~~ctiks~~   renas   shomromu   thosg

stick

3 **Look at the pictures. Write the story.**

One day Rosy went into the forest.

CD 4 **29** **Listen and draw lines.**

Jane   Vicky   Paul   Fred

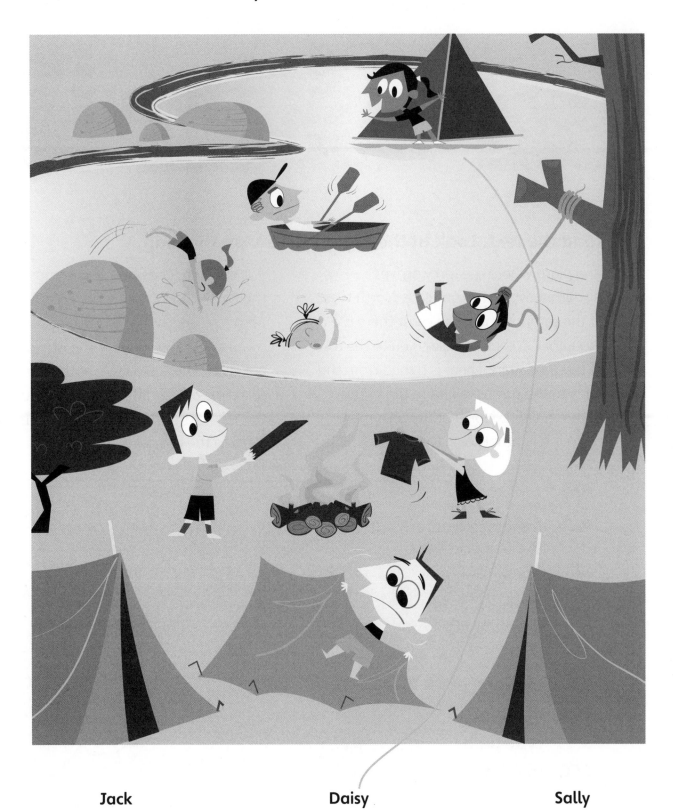

Jack   Daisy   Sally

1 **Look and write the words.**

a chair lift   cliffs   a cycle path   ~~a ferry~~

1 *a ferry*   2 _____   3 _____   4 _____

2 **Read the text. Look at the key and draw on the map.**

The place where the ferry arrives is south-west of the campsite. North-west of the campsite near the coast there is a mountain. A chair lift takes you to the top of the mountain. There is a road from the ferry to the campsite and to the bottom of the chair lift. North of the campsite there is a lighthouse on the coast.

A cycle path leads from the campsite to the lighthouse. There is another cycle path to a beach that is north-east of the campsite. In the south of the island there are cliffs. There is a cycle path from the campsite to the cliffs. In the south-east there is a farm. There is a road from the farm to the campsite.

Key

X   the place where the ferry arrives

M   the mountain

O   the bottom of the chair lift

- - - -   roads

L   the lighthouse

F   the farm

. . . .   cycle paths

CCC   the cliffs

1 **Look at Mia's map. Read, draw, measure and answer.**

What's the distance by road from:

1 … Mia's house to her school?   about _950_ metres
2 … Mia's house to the station?   about ____ metres
3 … Mia's house to the supermarket?   about ____ metres
4 … the swimming pool to the station?   about ____ metres
5 … the supermarket to the library?   about ____ metres

2 **Read and write _t_ (true) or _f_ (false).**

1 Mia's house is about 800 m from Peter's house.   [f]
2 Peter's house is about 600 m from the swimming pool.   [ ]
3 Mia has to walk further to school than Peter.   [ ]
4 The library is further from the school than it is from the swimming pool. [ ]
5 The station is closer to the supermarket than it is to the library. [ ]

1 **Match the questions with the answers.**

1 What are your holiday plans, Charlotte?

a ☐ No, we're going to a campsite near the sea.

2 Where do they live?

b ☐ 1 In the first week of the holidays, I'm going to visit my grandparents.

3 And what are you going to do there?

c ☐ I'm going to France with my parents.

4 What are you going to do afterwards?

d ☐ No, I'm going to learn to surf. My mum is going to teach me.

5 Are you going to stay in a hotel?

e ☐ In Ireland.

6 So are you going to swim all day?

f ☐ My grandparents have a farm and I'm going to look after the dogs and the pony.

2 **Look at Activity 1. Underline the mistakes. Then write the correct sentences.**

Charlotte is going to visit her uncle and aunt. They have a hotel in Spain. There she is going to look after the cows. Then she is going to France with her brother. There she is going to build sandcastles all day. In France Charlotte is going to stay at a hotel.

Charlotte is going to visit her grandparents.

_____

_____

_____

_____

3 **Write about your holiday plans.**

This summer I'm going …

1 (Think!) **Which one is different in each group? Look, think and circle.**

1

2

3

2 **Look and draw lines to make sentences.**

1 How	little	bread	do we	need?
	much	eggs	are we	needs?
	many	egg	are there	needing?

2 Would	he	like	a packet of	water?
	she	likes	a bottle of	crisps?
	you	liked	a bar of	chocolate?

3 How	many	milk	are there	on the table?
	much	chocolate	is there	next to the chair?
	old	books	there is	in the fridge?

4 Can I	has	a can	about	lemonade, please?
	had	a packet	in	milk, please?
	have	a glass of	of	crisps, please?

1 In the museum

Colour your favourite lessons.

- singing the song
- acting out our Egyptian cat play
- reading the Explorers story
- writing an advert
- reading *The secret of the Egyptian cat*
- learning about museums

Word focus Write three new words.

_____ _____ _____

Grammar focus Write two sentences about yourself.

_____

_____

Now tell a friend what you liked and didn't like in Unit 1.

2 The world around us

Colour your favourite lessons.

- singing the song
- finding out about our free time
- reading the Explorers story
- learning about life in art
- writing about my favourite outdoor place

Word focus Write three new words.

_____ _____ _____

Grammar focus Write two sentences about yourself.

_____

_____

Now tell a friend what you liked and didn't like in Unit 2.

3 Danger!

Colour your favourite lessons.

- singing the song
- acting out our emergency services play
- reading the Explorers story
- reading *The day the sea went out*
- writing a story about an accident
- learning about fire safety

Word focus Write three new words.

_____ _____ _____

Grammar focus Write two sentences about yourself.

_____

_____

Now tell a friend what you liked and didn't like in Unit 3.

Two return tickets

Colour your favourite lessons.

singing the song

reading the Explorers story

acting out our ticket office play

learning about forces

writing a notice for a school board

Word focus Write three new words.

Grammar focus Write two sentences about yourself.

Now tell a friend what you liked and didn't like in Unit 4.

 # Police!

Colour your favourite lessons.

singing the song

reading the Explorers story

reading *Yatin and the orange tree*

learning about crime fiction

finding out about our reading habits

writing a book review

Word focus Write three new words.

Grammar focus Write two sentences about yourself.

Now tell a friend what you liked and didn't like in Unit 5.

 # Mythical beasts

Colour your favourite lessons.

singing the song

reading the Explorers story

learning about predators and prey

acting out our unusual animal play

drawing and writing about an imaginary beast

Word focus Write three new words.

Grammar focus Write two sentences about yourself.

Now tell a friend what you liked and didn't like in Unit 6.

7 Orchestra practice

Colour your favourite lessons.

Word focus Write three new words.

- singing the song
- finding out about music in our class
- reading the Explorers story
- writing about my favourite band or singer
- reading *The bear's dream*
- learning about how we make sounds

_____ _____ _____

Grammar focus Write two sentences about yourself.

_____

_____

Now tell a friend what you liked and didn't like in Unit 7.

8 In the planetarium

Colour your favourite lessons.

Word focus Write three new words.

- singing the song
- acting out our interview with an alien
- reading the Explorers story
- learning about the solar system
- writing a space diary entry

_____ _____ _____

Grammar focus Write two sentences about yourself.

_____

_____

Now tell a friend what you liked and didn't like in Unit 8.

9 At the campsite

Colour your favourite lessons.

Word focus Write three new words.

- singing the song
- finding out about our holiday plans
- reading the Explorers story
- reading *The snares in the forest*
- writing a holiday leaflet
- learning about map reading

_____ _____ _____

Grammar focus Write two sentences about yourself.

_____

_____

Now tell a friend what you liked and didn't like in Unit 9.